JONATHAN TOEWS

by Tracy Nelson Maurer

Gail Saunders-Smith, PhD, Consulting Editor

CAPSTONE PRESS
a capstone imprint

Pebble Books are published by Capstone Press,
1710 Roe Crest Drive, North Mankato, Minnesota 56003
www.capstonepub.com

Library of Congress Cataloging-in-Publication Data
Maurer, Tracy, 1965–
 Jonathan Toews / by Tracy Nelson Maurer.
    pages cm.—(Pebble Books. Famous athletes)
 Includes bibliographical references and index.
ISBN 978-1-4914-6235-5 (library binding : alk. paper)
ISBN 978-1-4914-6251-5 (ebook pdf)
ISBN 978-1-4914-6255-3 (pebble books pbk. : alk. paper)
1. Jonathan Toews, 1991– —Juvenile literature. 2. Hockey players—United States—
Biography—Juvenile literature. I. Title.
 GV865.T73M38 2016
 796.357092—dc23
 [B]   2015001861

Note to Parents and Teachers

The Famous Athletes supports national curriculum standards for
social studies related to people, places, and culture. This book
describes and illustrates Jonathan Toews. The images support
early readers in understanding the text. The repetition of words
and phrases helps early readers learn new words. This book also
introduces early readers to subject-specific vocabulary words,
which are defined in the Glossary section. Early readers may need
assistance to read some words and to use the Table of Contents,
Glossary, Read More, Internet Sites, and Index sections of the book.

Printed in the United States of America in Brainerd, Minnesota
042015   008826BANGF15

TABLE OF CONTENTS

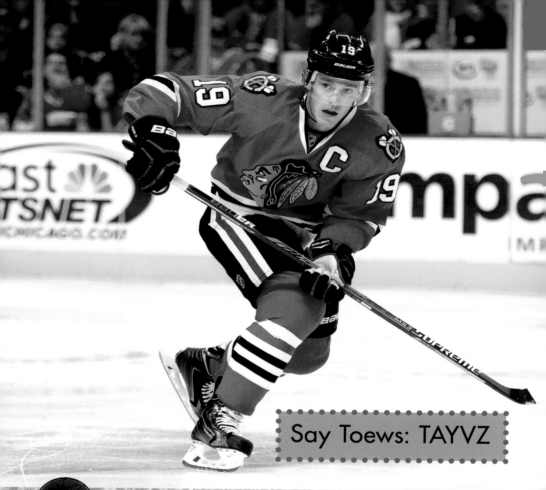

Say Toews: TAYVZ

1988

born in
Winnipeg,
Manitoba

SKATING STAR

NHL star Jonathan Bryan Toews

was born April 29, 1988.

His father, Bryan, first strapped

ice skates on Jonathan at age 3.

By age 5 Jonathan was

a very good skater.

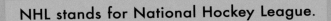

NHL stands for National Hockey League.

Children skate on an outdoor ice rink.

1988

born in
Winnipeg,
Manitoba

Jonathan loved playing outdoors in Canada.

In winter his parents built a backyard ice rink.

Jonathan and his brother, David, played ice hockey for hours.

1988

2003–2005

born in
Winnipeg,
Manitoba

attends
Shattuck-
St. Mary's
School

At age 15 Jonathan left Canada to go to Shattuck-St. Mary's in Minnesota. The high school's hockey team has won many championships. Jonathan's team won in 2005.

1988 — born in Winnipeg, Manitoba

2003–2005 — attends Shattuck–St. Mary's School

2005–2007 — attends University of North Dakota

After high school Jonathan went to college in North Dakota. He led the school's hockey team to the national playoffs in 2006 and 2007.

 12

1988
born in Winnipeg, Manitoba

2003–2005
attends Shattuck-St. Mary's School

2005–2007
attends University of North Dakota

2006
signs with the Chicago Blackhawks

NHL SUPERSTAR

The Chicago Blackhawks chose

Jonathan in the 2006 NHL Draft.

He joined the team the next year.

He was 19. He scored his first

NHL goal on his first shot

in his first game!

1988	2003–2005	2005–2007	2006	2008
born in Winnipeg, Manitoba	attends Shattuck-St. Mary's School	attends University of North Dakota	signs with the Chicago Blackhawks	becomes team captain at age 20

Jonathan shined as the team's center. He was a leader on the ice. The Blackhawks made him team captain in 2008. In 2010 he helped the team win the Stanley Cup.

2010
helps the Blackhawks win first Stanley Cup since 1961

1988	**2003–2005**	**2005–2007**	**2006**	**2008**
born in Winnipeg, Manitoba	attends Shattuck-St. Mary's School	attends University of North Dakota	signs with the Chicago Blackhawks	becomes team captain at age 20

Jonathan earned a spot on Canada's Olympic hockey team in 2010. His team won the gold medal. In 2014 Jonathan and Team Canada won the gold medal again.

2010 helps the Blackhawks win first Stanley Cup since 1961

2010 wins Olympic gold medal

1988	**2003–2005**	**2005–2007**	**2006**	**2008**
born in Winnipeg, Manitoba	attends Shattuck-St. Mary's School	attends University of North Dakota	signs with the Chicago Blackhawks	becomes team captain at age 20

Jonathan and the Blackhawks won the Stanley Cup again in 2013. The next season the Blackhawks tried to win back-to-back titles. But they lost in the semifinals.

2010
helps the Blackhawks win first Stanley Cup since 1961

2010
wins Olympic gold medal

2013
helps the Blackhawks win the Stanley Cup

2014
wins Olympic gold medal

Jonathan Toews

1988
born in Winnipeg, Manitoba

2003–2005
attends Shattuck-St. Mary's School

2005–2007
attends University of North Dakota

2006
signs with the Chicago Blackhawks

2008
becomes team captain at age 20

LOOKING AHEAD

In 2015 Jonathan led his team
to another Stanley Cup.
He has led winning teams
ever since he learned to skate.
Jonathan plans to help his team
win for many more seasons.

2010
helps the
Blackhawks win
first Stanley Cup
since 1961

2010
wins
Olympic
gold
medal

2013
helps the
Blackhawks
win the
Stanley Cup

2014
wins
Olympic
gold medal

2015
helps the
Blackhawks
win the
Stanley Cup

21

GLOSSARY

back-to-back—two in a row

captain—the player on the team who is the leader; the captain wears the letter "C" on his jersey

center—a skater who mainly plays in the middle of the ice

draft—an event held for teams to choose new people to play for them

season—the time of year in which NHL hockey games are played

semifinal—the round of games that decides which team goes on to compete for the championship

Stanley Cup—the trophy given to the team that wins the NHL championship

title—the championship of a league

CRITICAL THINKING USING THE COMMON CORE

1. Jonathan had a backyard ice rink as a child. How might this have helped him become a good hockey player? (Integration of Knowledge and Ideas)

2. Read the text on page 15. Then look at the photograph on page 14. What is Jonathan holding? (Craft and Structure)